lpers

Nurses

by Cari Meister

Bullfrog
Books

Ideas for Parents and Teachers

Bullfrog Books let children practice reading informational text at the earliest reading levels. Repetition, familiar words, and photo labels support early readers.

Before Reading

- Discuss the cover photo. What does it tell them?

- Look at the picture glossary together. Read and discuss the words.

Read the Book

- "Walk" through the book and look at the photos. Let the child ask questions. Point out the photo labels.

- Read the book to the child, or have him or her read independently.

After Reading

- Prompt the child to think more. Ask: Have you ever met a nurse? What did the nurse do for you?

Bullfrog Books are published by Jump!
5357 Penn Avenue South
Minneapolis, MN 55419
www.jumplibrary.com

Library of Congress Cataloging-in-Publication Data
Meister, Cari.
  Nurses / by Cari Meister.
    pages cm.—(Community helpers)
  Summary: "This photo-illustrated book for early readers describes what nurses do in the clinic, hospital, or emergency room and how they work to help keep us healthy and well"—Provided by publisher.
  Includes index.
  ISBN 978-1-62031-094-6 (hardcover)
  ISBN 978-1-62496-162-5 (ebook)
  ISBN 978-1-62031-138-7 (paperback)
  1. Nursing—Juvenile literature. 2. Nurses—Juvenile literature. I. Title.
  RT61.5.M45 2015
  610.73—dc23

                                    2013042373

Editor: Wendy Dieker
Series Designer: Ellen Huber
Book Designer: Lindaanne Donohoe
Photo Researcher: Kurtis Kinneman

Photo Credits: All photos by Shutterstock except Getty 4, 7, 21; iStock 12-13, 16; Corbis 18-19; Superstock 6-7, 16-17, 22; ChameleonsEye 23

Printed in the United States of America at Corporate Graphics, North Mankato, Minnesota.
6-2014
10 9 8 7 6 5 4 3 2 1

Table of Contents

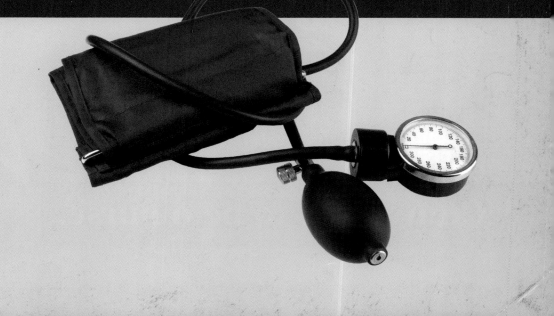

Nurses at Work

Cam wants to be a nurse.

What do they do?

They care for people.

Gil fell off his bike.

Ouch!

He has a bad cut.
Ina cleans it.

Jo has a sore throat.

Sue checks it.

She uses a
long swab.

Say, "Ahhh!"

swabs

Ann needs surgery.

Kim helps her get ready.

She puts in an IV.

IV

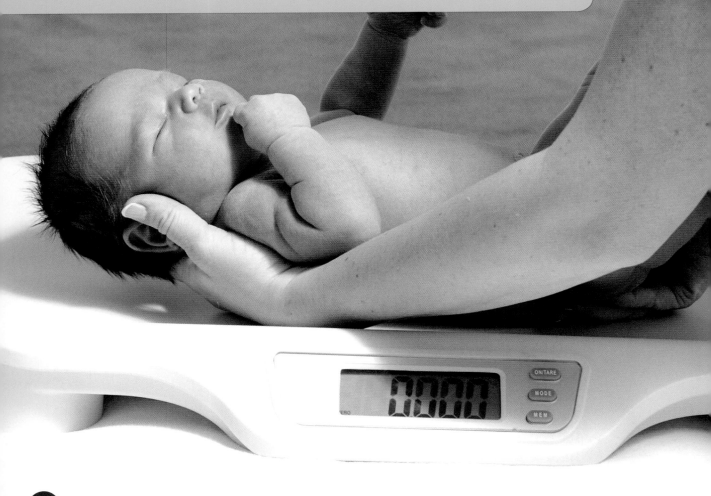

Nurse Jody works with babies.
She weighs Ben.

Is he growing?
Yes. He is!

Dan gives
Wes a shot.

It protects him
from disease.

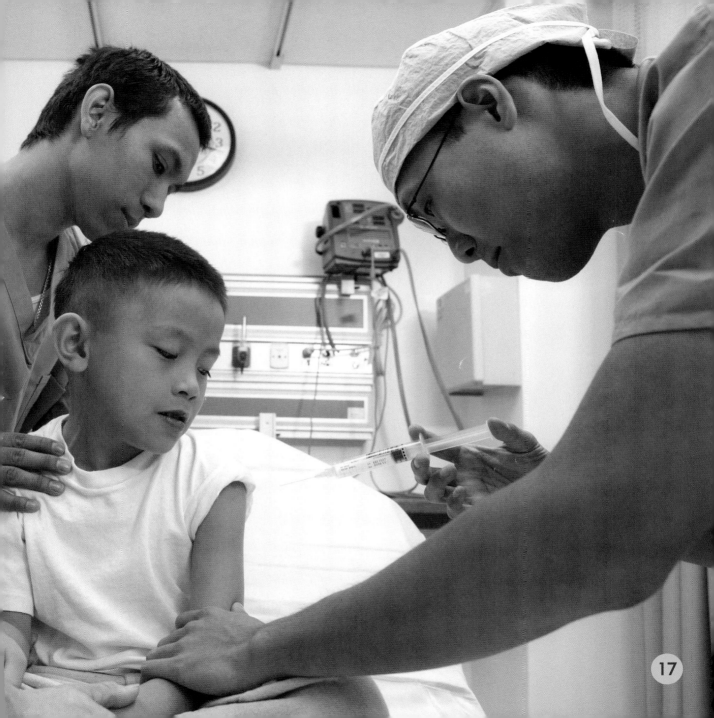

Dot works in the emergency room.

She works fast.

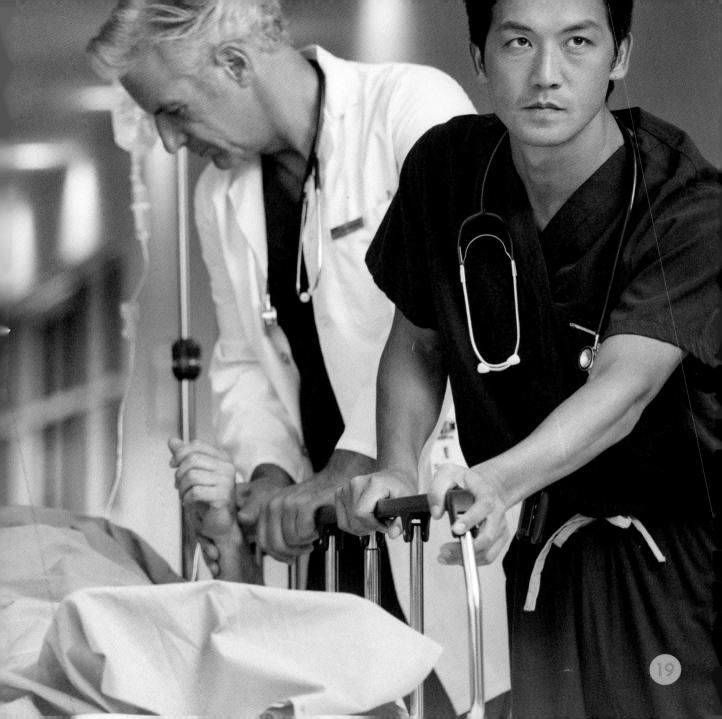

Nurses keep us well!

At the Clinic

blood pressure cuff
A machine that measures how hard a person's blood pumps.

exam table
A table where patients sit while being examined by a nurse or doctor.

scale
A machine used for weighing people.

Picture Glossary

emergency room
A place where people go to get fast help after a bad accident or sudden illness.

surgery
When a doctor fixes something inside your body.

IV
A tube used to put medicine or other liquid directly into a person's veins.

swab
A stick with a piece of soft cotton on the end.

Index

To Learn More

Learning more is as easy as 1, 2, 3.

1) Go to www.factsurfer.com

2) Enter "nurses" into the search box.

3) Click the "Surf" button to see a list of websites.

With factsurfer.com, finding more information is just a click away.